NATURAL
DISASTERS

WILDFIRES

ABDO
Publishing Company

Rochelle Baltzer

Big Buddy **BOOKS**
Natural Disasters

VISIT US AT
www.abdopublishing.com

Published by ABDO Publishing Company, 8000 West 78th Street, Edina, Minnesota 55439.

Printed in the United States of America, North Mankato, Minnesota.
052011
092011

 PRINTED ON RECYCLED PAPER

Coordinating Series Editor: Sarah Tieck
Contributing Editors: Megan M. Gunderson, BreAnn Rumsch, Marcia Zappa
Graphic Design: Adam Craven
Cover Photograph: *iStockphoto*: ©iStockphoto.com/Byronsdad.
Interior Photographs/Illustrations: *AP Photo*: Evan Collis/FESA (p. 11), Kevork Djansezian (p. 21), Damian
    Dovarganes (p. 11), Robin Loznak/Daily Inter Lake (p. 13), Ben Margot (p. 23), North Wind Picture Archives
    via AP Images (p. 25), Sue Ogrocki (p. 15), Erik Petersen/Bozeman Daily Chronicle (p. 19), Jack Smith (p. 15),
    Mark J. Terrill (p. 17); *Photo Researchers, Inc.*: David R. Frazier Photolibrary, Inc. (p. 30); *Shutterstock*: George
    Burba (pp. 9, 29), HelgaChirkova (p. 9), Elanamiv (p. 9), Arnold John Labrentz (p. 7), Vladimir Meinkov (p. 5),
    Thomas_Ondrejka (p. 21), robootb (p. 25); *Wisconsin Historical Society* (p. 27).

Library of Congress Cataloging-in-Publication Data

Baltzer, Rochelle, 1982-
  Wildfires / Rochelle Baltzer.
      p. cm. -- (Natural disasters)
  ISBN 978-1-61783-036-5
  1. Wildfires--Juvenile literature. I. Title.
  SD421.23.B35 2012
  363.34'9--dc23
                    2011013148

WILDFIRES

CONTENTS

RAGING FLAMES

The ground is cracked and thirsty. Hot wind blows through the trees, moving piles of dry leaves. Lightning flashes and a fire sparks. All of a sudden, flames spread across the land. It's a wildfire!

A wildfire is a natural disaster. Natural disasters happen because of weather or changes inside Earth. They can cause much **damage** and even take lives. By learning about them, people are better able to stay safe.

Wildfires can spread at speeds up to 14 miles (23 km) per hour!

WHAT IS A WILDFIRE?

A wildfire is an uncontrolled fire in a forest, grassland, or other wild area. Wildfires can spread to farms and towns. Ground fires, surface fires, and crown fires are types of wildfires.

Ground fires burn on or below ground. They move across soil and roots. Surface fires burn near the ground in grass, bushes, and tree trunks. Crown fires spread across the tops of bushes and trees.

A wildfire can burn everything in its path. This includes trees, plants, homes, and even people and animals.

PERFECT CONDITIONS

A fire needs heat, **fuel**, and oxygen (AHK-sih-juhn) to burn. These three things make up the fire triangle. When one of these is taken away, a fire stops.

Heat for a wildfire can come from lightning. It can also come from trash fires or campfires. Fuel can be trees, grasses, and anything that can start on fire. Oxygen is a gas found in the air.

BREAKING NEWS

During dry storms, lightning is more likely to start fires. No rain hits the ground. So, there is no water to slow or stop a fire.

THE FIRE TRIANGLE

Fuel

Oxygen

Heat

Wildfires often occur after **droughts**. Droughts dry out natural **fuels**, such as grass and trees. This makes them burn easily and quickly.

Hot wind also dries out fuels. And, it brings in more oxygen. In Southern California, the Santa Ana winds make conditions right for wildfires. These hot, dry winds blow across land in fall and winter.

BREAKING NEWS

Many harmful US wildfires occur in Montana, Idaho, Wyoming, Washington, Colorado, Oregon, and California.

Wildfires happen around the world. In Australia, they are often called bushfires.

In October 2007, the Santa Ana winds made California wildfires powerful. The fires destroyed more than 1,000 homes.

FANNING THE FLAMES

Wildfires spread at different speeds. On steep land, a fire usually spreads uphill very quickly. That's because as fire burns, heat rises up. It preheats **fuel** in the fire's path. This makes the fuel catch fire quickly and easily.

The amount of wind also affects how fast a wildfire spreads. Wind moves heat along. This makes a fire quickly spread and grow. It can also make it change direction.

Wildfires often spread quickly on slopes with lots of plants and trees.

FIGHTING BACK

When a wildfire is burning out of control, firefighters work to put it out. This is unsafe work, so firefighters are well trained.

Some wildfires are in places that are hard to reach. Special firefighters called smoke jumpers ride in airplanes or helicopters to these spots. Then, they jump out from high in the air and get to work!

BREAKING NEWS

A wildfire may run into water or get rained on. This can make it stop on its own.

Firefighters wear special gear to keep their bodies safe.

A parachute fans out like an umbrella to slow a smoke jumper's fall.

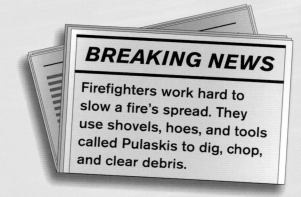

Firefighters work to remove **fuel**, heat, and oxygen from a wildfire. They clear away leaves, twigs, and other **debris** from the fire's path. This slows the fire. They also spray water or **chemicals** on the fire. This cools and slows it.

Sometimes, firefighters set a new fire to control a wildfire. This is called a backfire. It is closely controlled to burn fuel in a wildfire's path. This can stop the wildfire from spreading.

Airplanes and helicopters dump water and chemicals to slow or stop wildfires.

17

AFTER A WILDFIRE

In the wake of a wildfire, there is much cleanup. Workers shovel away ash and **debris**. People fix and rebuild **damaged** homes and other buildings.

A wildfire can leave land bare. Plants and trees that once held soil in place are burned. The weak land is more likely to experience **erosion** and **landslides**. Also, a wildfire can destroy animal homes and food sources.

After a wildfire, people plant new trees. The trees grow and make land stronger.

STAYING SAFE

Officials take steps to prevent wildfires from causing **damage**. In dry weather, they watch for fires from tall towers or airplanes. They also study past fires in an area.

Sometimes, officials start fires to prevent fires! They use fire to remove **fuel** from areas that are likely to catch fire. This is called a prescribed fire. Officials closely control it so it does not become a wildfire.

If wildfires are likely, officials may not allow campfires (*left*). Or, they may close a forest to the public (*above*).

Still, wildfires start and spread fast in the right conditions. So, people who live where they are common stay prepared. During a wildfire, they may have to leave their homes.

Most wildfires are started by people. To avoid this, people must be smart about building campfires. They should build them in open areas. And, they should make sure a fire is completely out before leaving.

Since 1944, Smokey Bear has made people more aware of wildfire safety.

CASE STUDY:
PESHTIGO FIRE

The small mining town of Peshtigo, Wisconsin, had a dry summer and fall in 1871. At that time, farmers used fire to clear land. Also, loggers and railroad workers burned leftover **debris** from cutting down trees.

Small fires from these practices were burning on the night of October 8. A windstorm blew the fires together, forming a giant wildfire.

The Peshtigo fire (*above*) was on the same day as the Great Chicago Fire (*below*). The Chicago fire was not a wildfire, but it is much more well known.

AREAS OF FIRE

MICHIGAN

Peshtigo

LAKE MICHIGAN

WISCONSIN

ILLINOIS
Chicago

The fire moved so fast that people didn't have much warning. Some survived by waiting in a river. Peshtigo burned, as did other small towns in northern Wisconsin and Michigan.

The Peshtigo fire was the worst wildfire in US history. Including areas near Peshtigo, about 1,200 people died. More than 1 million acres (400,000 ha) of land burned.

During the fire, thick smoke made it hard to see even a few feet ahead.

PESHTIGO FIRE CEMETERY

On the night of October 8, 1871, Peshtigo, a booming town of 1700 people, was wiped out of existence in the greatest forest fire disaster in American history.

Loss of life and even property in the great fire occurring the same night in Chicago did not match the death toll and destruction visited upon northeastern Wisconsin during the same dreadful hours.

The town of Peshtigo was centered around a woodenware factory, the largest in the country. Every building in the community was lost. The tornado of fire claimed at least 800 lives in this area. Many of the victims lie here. The memory of 350 unidentified men, women, and children is preserved in a nearby mass grave.

Erected in 1951 by the people of Peshtigo.

Today, people visit Peshtigo to learn about the fire. They remember the lives lost.

FORCE OF NATURE

Wildfires can cause much **damage**. But they also make room for new trees to grow by clearing land. And they burn dead or sick plants, which improves forests.

Wildfires will always happen. Learning more about them helps people find new ways to be safe and prevent damage. This can save lives!

Prescribed fires burn dead plants. Limiting these fuels lowers the chances of a wildfire starting or spreading.

NEWS FLASH!

- People cause more than four out of five wildfires.

- Every year, wildfires clear about 5 million acres (2 million ha) of US land.

- Animals have a natural sense for danger. When they sense fire, many leave an area. Others hide in dens or other shelters.

- Trees can explode during a wildfire! This is because some trees make oils that catch fire very easily.

IMPORTANT WORDS

chemical (KEH-mih-kuhl) a substance that can cause reactions and changes.

damage (DA-mihj) harm or injury.

debris (duh-BREE) bits and pieces of something broken down or wrecked.

drought (DRAUT) a long period of dry weather.

erosion (ih-ROH-zhuhn) wearing away of the land often caused by water or wind.

fuel (FYOOL) something burned to give heat or power.

landslide a mass of soil or rock that slides down a slope.

WEB SITES

To learn more about wildfires, visit ABDO Publishing Company online. Web sites about wildfires are featured on our Book Links page. These links are routinely monitored and updated to provide the most current information available.

www.abdopublishing.com

INDEX